*Short Story Bible Study Series*

# The Perfect Couple

## and Other Stories

SO-FAE-375

## Study Guide

**by Donald L. Deffner**
**Earl H. Gaulke, Editor**

Publishing House
St. Louis

*To*
*a very patient woman*
*my wife Corinne*

Copyright © 1993 Concordia Publishing House
3558 South Jefferson Avenue, St. Louis, MO 63118-3968
Manufactured in the United States of America

# CONTENTS

# ABOUT THIS BOOK

Everyone loves a story!

In India a native evangelist has a bicycle, a lantern, and a drum. He goes into a village, people gather at the sound of the drum, and he tells them a story. It is the story of Jesus.

Jesus Himself told stories.

> Jesus used parables to tell all these things to the crowds; he would not say a thing to them without using a parable. (Matthew 13:34 TEV)

He would say, "A certain man was going down from Jerusalem to Jericho, when robbers attacked him . . . " (Luke 10:30). And a hearer mentally responded, *Yes, Rabbi, why I know just what you are talking about! Why, Uncle Daniel was attacked on that road just last week!*

Jesus followed the principle of going "from the known to the unknown." He started with the real world of his hearers and then moved on to the theological truth involved.

Martin Luther wrote:

> Without knowledge of literature pure theology cannot at all endure . . . I see that there has never been a great revelation of the Word of God unless He has first prepared the way by the rise and prosperity of languages and letters, as though they were John the Baptists . . .

In *Theology and Modern Literature,* Amon Wilder held that in humanity's effort at self-understanding we need cultural images, works of art. Literature assists us in this search for self-understanding. "Philosophy and theology as rational disciplines are inadequate to the process."

And Italian novelist Ignazio Silone in "The Choice of Companions" mused:

> The spiritual condition I have described allows of no boasting
> . . . . It resembles a camp of refugees in some no man's land,
> out in the open, existing by chance. What do you expect refu-
> gees to do from morning to night? They spend the best part of
> their time telling each other their stories. The stories are not
> very entertaining, to be sure, but they tell them anyhow—
> mainly, to understand what has happened.

Story is also receiving a revival in preaching today. Homiletician Charles Rice says, "The way towards renewal of preaching is to be found in the recovery of storytelling." Indeed, *the Bible is story*. Along with this has come an emphasis on the preacher's valid use (reflexive and self-insightful, not subjective) of "My Story" from the.preacher's own faith-walk. This is then related to God's Story (the Gospel) and correlated with The People's Story—their own Christian life.

Children often say, "Tell me a story!" I believe I told my children the story about Hansel and Gretel one thousand times. They couldn't wait for the moment when the wicked witch would say, "And now I am going to throw you into my oven! *Boo!*" And then I would hug them.

A seminary student recounts a class of junior high students he taught. Bedlam reigned. Then he said, "Say, I'd like to tell you a story." Suddenly silence fell over the group. They settled down and listened attentively. He couldn't believe the change that had taken place, he said.

And stories also enliven adult Bible classes and home discussion groups. Our involvement in the characters' lives can quicken and enrich our concern for the issue involved—pride, gossip, loneliness, witnessing, etc.—and assist us as Christians in grappling with the question (as Francis Schaeffer puts it) "How should we then live?"

The following stories are offered as an issue-oriented resource for adult Bible study and discussion groups.

There are two 6-session courses, each session based on 1 to 3 short stories, arranged topically according to thematic issues, with discussion questions referencing Bible texts designed to lead the learner to apply Scripture to his/her own life. These are for use with small home-discussion groups or in the Sunday morning or weekday church Bible class. Additionally, the study booklets can simply be used by individuals—for their own individual reading, meditation, and spiritual nourishment.

Because the story/stories for each session can be read in an average of 9 minutes (range, 5 to 13 minutes), the stories may be read at the time of meeting—either silently by each participant before discussion or orally by volunteer readers in the group. A third alternative is that the stories be read beforehand.

Also, the stories can be shared with people outside the church. Note the Appendix (which can be used as the discussion starter) for "The Perfect Couple."

Indeed, "tell me *your* story" can be a fruitful catalyst in reaching out to others as we first *actively listen* to *them.* But then something else may occur. As J. Russell Hale, author of *Who Are the Unchurched,* says,

> Your tone of voice, gestures, etc., are very important as you say, "I'd like to have you tell me your story about what you think of the church. Go back to your childhood" *And they really open up.*
>
> If you listen when they tell you their story, a point will come when they'll say, "Tell me your story." And you don't hand out tracts, but as the two stories converge there is the miracle of dialog, the point when *God's story* can come out . . . And the "rumor of angels" impinges on their ordinary experiences.

In whatever setting you use this book, may the Holy Spirit attend your reading. And then, may you be moved to share with others *The Story.*

Besides the discussion questions for each session, here are key questions to consider throughout the course:

1. Is the story true to life? Give reasons for your answer.
2. What, if anything, does the story have to say to our Christian faith and life?
3. How does it reveal or point to our need? (Law)
4. How does it point to or suggest God's action for us in Christ? (Gospel)

# SESSION 1
# Forgiveness

## The Perfect Couple

Well, it was just the perfect night for the occasion. And for the perfect couple—Harry and Betsy Anderson—celebrating a 50th wedding anniversary. They were loved and praised and admired by the whole congregation. Tonight the parish would honor them with a festive banquet—and make it a celebration they would always remember.

Janice Klappermeier, tireless church worker, came out of the church kitchen and surveyed the banquet hall. With the back of her left wrist she wiped the sweat off her forehead, as the heady aroma of fresh-baked ham and sweet perking coffee made her smile. She smelled the honeysuckle centerpieces. She saw the men in multicolored outfits ready to serve the dinner.

The Ladies Aid had really outdone itself tonight. Lacy baby's breath and lily of the valley were delicately laid around each place setting. The parish hall would be full— they had guessed within 10 of the 290 people now milling around waiting for Pastor Schultz's opening prayer. He was there, with his usual gentle manner, moving from one little knot of people to another, with his smile and nod and handshake. Even old Mrs. Feuerabend had made it out tonight and was demonstrating her collapsible cane, the one with the gold handle, to a group of admiring youngsters.

Janice Klappermeier, arms akimbo, gave a self-satisfied "humph!" and swished back into the kitchen.

Ed Larsen, the emcee, always kept things moving along nicely. The desserts had just been served. He started the round of brief speeches and little gifts and mementos that were showered on the Andersons. Among them was a heavy bronze plaque—a wreath with a cross in the middle—and the words "Fifty Years in Our Lord." It was duplicated by a large flowered wreath of the same design right behind the head table, where the couple sat with Ed and his wife, and Pastor and Mrs. Schultz.

Gradually, the children left the hall for an adjacent room to watch a movie. Soon the banquet hall rang with applause as speaker after speaker praised the Andersons, their long and varied church service, their devotion to their family, and their evident love for each other. Ed neatly summed it up, everybody agreed, just before he asked Harry Anderson to say a few words, when he concluded, "And so, I think I can say for all of us here tonight, I'd call them—Harry and Betsy—'the perfect couple.' "

Well, this time you'd thought the applause would never stop. All were on their feet smiling as they clapped. But finally the applause did stop, as Harry got up and gently waved everyone to sit down.

"This means an awful lot to Betsy and me," he began. "And we thank you. For the wonderful meal . . . " He nodded towards the Ladies Aid and the men waiters, "for your many kind gifts, for your presence here. For all your love. We truly thank you."

But then Harry paused, and looked over the heads of the crowd, seemingly far away. He began again, slowly. "But what I'm going to say now you might not like to hear, but I've got to say it. That is, Betsy and I have got to say it."

Harry took a short, tight breath. "We've talked about this and she knows what I'm going to do . . . " Even Ed Larsen couldn't avoid taking a puzzled, sidelong glance at Betsy, sitting next to him and nodding silently. Her eyes stayed on her lap, where she was tracing the border of her napkin with her thumb and forefinger.

"More than 50 years ago Betsy and I married each other—each for the wrong reasons. The first years were

10

touch and go. We often talked of divorce—indeed have done so over the years . . . " The hall was hushed now except for Helen Schlaegel clearing her throat occasionally. (She always did that when she got nervous.) At Harry's word *divorce,* several couples in the large hall made a point of not looking at each other.

Harry continued, "Oh, we went to church and all that, but our religion was not at the center of our lives, or our marriage, at all. But that's not the real point. You folks here have been such great friends, but you honor us too much. You have spoken of us as the perfect couple." Again he sighed quickly. "But we're not.

"In the early years of our marriage . . . " He paused again until he saw Betsy's nod. "In the early years of our marriage, Betsy had an affair with one of my best friends."

Suzy Ottermeier, who had managed to find a second helping of strawberry shortcake with whipped cream, and who almost had a huge piece halfway to her mouth, suddenly dropped her fork with a loud clatter. As several dozen pairs of eyes "shushed" her, she blushed and quickly looked toward Harry at the head table, where he continued.

"Well, I left Betsy for a while after that. Some time later I came back, but I really gave her a bad time. Those were rough years—and we made it rough on each other. Then, later, after Betsy's hysterectomy, I had an affair. And that just about ended our marriage. But here is where Pastor Schultz helped us so much. And we truly thank him." He nodded to the pastor, sitting on his right.

"We repeatedly failed each other—and despaired of our marriage. But—and that's my point—*we didn't give up.* We began—with Pastor's counsel, and with much soul-searching—to begin to learn—I guess really for the first time—the meaning of forgiveness. We discovered the healing power of the Eucharist as we knelt arm in arm at the altar every Sunday. We learned to pray together and to read our Bible together.

"At times we wanted to throw in the towel—especially when we felt like hypocrites with your praise of us all the time. We didn't know how to tell you what we really were like—what we'd been through—how we had botched our lives. And we felt we had failed our children. You know Mary is a psychiatrist, but Bill has been on drugs, and George has had two disastrous marriages.

"But by God's grace—and that's what Betsy and I want to say tonight . . . " (Harry's voice was hoarse now) "for God's sake, *keep on trying in your marriage*—in your acceptance of each other and in your acceptance of yourself, as God in Christ has accepted you.

"*Keep trying*—and keep on forgiving. The Holy Spirit will give you the strength . . . "

Harry paused. The hall was hushed. You could smell the honeysuckle. Betsy's hands now lay silent in her lap. "I guess that's all Betsy and I have to say. Thank you again. But don't think of us as 'perfect'—just *forgiven*."

There was a long silence. Helen Schlaegel cleared her throat again. A baby sneezed. Then somewhere in the large hall someone slowly clapped. Then the clapping soared and swelled and everyone was standing, crying and laughing. Harry saw Bill and Clara Harms—he knew about their problems—cautiously hug each other. And the clapping and the tears went on and on.

*Do you know of friends with whom you would like to share this story? Why not share it, including the Appendix.*

# South from Alaska

Doug and Doreen Evans glowed as they drove home from Denver to their apartment in Colorado Springs. Doug had just returned from a year's Army service in Alaska. It had been "the hard duty" as he called it. They held hands as he drove the old LTD with his left hand.

"I can't believe you're back, Doug," Doreen whispered.

"I can't either. You can't know the sense of relief I experienced when our planeload of troops finally left the ground. We cheered—and cried. One whole year out of our lives!

"What a rotten assignment!" he continued angrily. "One phone call to you a month. So I *was* special services. I'd rather have been in Europe all this year. What a godforsaken land up there—but I felt like I was in prison."

Doreen snuggled close. "Forget it, honey," she said, "at least for tonight. You're home. That's all that matters to me."

Doug sighed and eased the car off the freeway into Colorado Springs.

All the old memories flooded back. His family coming out to the Springs and Manitou from Russell, Kansas; being the first person in the family to see the familiar outline of Pike's Peak; viewing a herd of 200 elk at 11,000 feet one morning on Trail Ridge at 4 o'clock as Daddy "shot" them in color with his new camera.

But now—home again—in the Colorado Springs area he loved so much.

He'd been married two years ago. His wife had a good job. Then—bamb!—one year in Alaska.

"Doug! You're not listening to me!" Doreen chided softly. "You just missed our street!"

"Sorry, Hon." Doug backed up, made a quick U-turn, and soon they were in their apartment.

"Hurray!" he shouted as he entered.

"Honey, you kept it just the way I remembered it," Doug exclaimed.

"You knew I would. I love you, Doug. I always have."

Her voice trailed off as Doug assumed she was thinking back to the time she was 13 when she had first eyed him in junior high in Russell, Kansas, and had fallen hopelessly, forever in love.

"Oh, I forgot—" She headed for the kitchen. "Champagne for the conquering hero!"

"Conqueror of what?" he laughed. "The tundra? King crab from Kodiak?"

"Doug, Honey, come here. *I love you.*" Doreen drew him down onto the couch.

His dark mood disappeared. "Doreen, I love you, too, with all my heart. I always have. But there's one thing I've got to tell you, before, well, before we go any . . . well."

He rose and walked to the fireplace.

Fingering a football trophy on the mantel, he continued. "I've got to say it. You've always been so, so *honest* with me. I've got to get this off my chest, or I'll burst."

13

"It's okay, Doug," Doreen replied, mystified. "Here, Honey, your champagne. Relax. Remember—we've got *all night*. You don't have to be out at Fort Carson for three days. Relax, honey."

Doug remained where he was.

"There was this one night. Only once, mind you. We finally got a pass way down into Anchorage and all got boozed up on Fourth Avenue. Sleazy hotel. Just pick out your girl. Pay at the bar. She'll come to your room. Girl from the lower 48: $100. Native: $50.

"I did it," Doug confessed, pain clogging his voice. "I didn't want to, Doreen. But I was so lonely. I missed affection so much. The pictures of the *Playboy* girl of the month on the walls of the rec room on post bugged me. Each guy had 'his' month of return to the 'lower 48' pegged with that girl of the month. My month was November."

Guilt-filled, Doug rambled on apologizing. "Well, the girl came to my room. I was half-bombed—later I showed her out. I felt so ashamed. I read a Gideon Bible the rest of the night."

He paused. "I'm sorry . . . truly sorry. Will you forgive me? I don't know what happened to me. It wasn't *me*."

He paused, fearful of her response.

Doreen set down her champagne, rose and walked over to the fireplace.

"I don't want to say this badly," she began.

Doug froze. Dear God! he thought. I can't lose her now! Why didn't I just shut up? I wanted so much to be honest with her. To "clear the decks" as we always had.

"Doug," Doreen began slowly. "You know I'm not good with words. I believe what you did was wrong . . . "

She groaned and looked toward the ceiling. "I understand. You don't need to ask for *my* forgiveness. Ask for God's. I do every day.

"Doug," she continued, "I love you. I've always loved you. That's all I can say . . . Doug, please . . . "

Doug hesitantly met Doreen halfway across the room and slowly embraced her. As he did, he felt her stiffen.

"Should I or shouldn't I?" she asked calmly, as if she wasn't talking to him—Doug Evans, Army man, tough/tender guy.

"Should you what?" Doug asked benignly, beginning to feel the effects of the champagne.

"Sit down, honey," Doreen said softly.

They watched the first crackle in the fireplace for a moment. They snuggled close together. Doug felt great. Home at last. Doreen! What a girl. And she had accepted him. Thank God! Never again. Good-bye, Alaska!

"Doug?" Doreen moved closer.

"Yayus?" he said, in his old joking manner.

She paused. "I was lonely, too. There was one time—"

Now *Doug* stiffened.

"It was so gosh-awful desolate here. You said the Army wives got cabin fever in Alaska. I did too—even though I went to all the events planned on the post . . . "

Doug didn't move. He didn't want to hear what might be coming.

The silence was deafening.

Doreen was direct. He could say that for her.

"It was just *one* time, after a party. I hadn't heard your voice or received a letter for three weeks. I was *so* lonely. I met this guy and he reminded me of you. We made out. But all the time I was thinking of *you*. It was *you* I was . . . well, not making love to . . . it wasn't that." Doreen's voice faded away.

It seemed like an hour before Doreen said, "Doug, I'm truly sorry."

Two inert bodies sat on the couch as candles and fireplace flickered. The champagne grew warm, then dead.

Doug rose and stumbled toward the door. "How could you? I *trusted* you!" he shouted angrily. "You had everything you needed! My monthly check, your friends at the post. You knew you were the only one for me." His voice trailed off, and so did he as he staggered out the apartment door, slamming it shut.

Sometimes time does not pass. Sometimes it ellipses. And though an hour had gone by, Doreen felt it was like one minute when Doug returned. In a broken voice, he asked, "Doreen, will you forgive me?"

She was sitting swollen-eyed on the couch where he had left her.

Their eyes reminded each other that they were people of very few words. They had always made love with their bodies—never talking, not with oh's and ah's and promises.

"If God forgives us, why can't we forgive each other?" Doreen said, weeping.

"We can." Doug answered solemnly.

And that night, they did not make love. They just lay in each other's arms.

Sometimes he stroked her hair. Sometimes she kissed his lips lightly.

And, finally, they both drifted off to sleep, arms entwined, until morning.

# Talking about . . . Forgiveness

A woman came to a pastor's home late one night. She was pregnant, but her husband had been impotent for 10 years. It was a small town, and the whole town knew of his problem.

What to do? Tell her husband of her unfaithfulness to him with another man? They prayed over it, long and agonizingly.

Finally she decided to tell her husband. He forgave her. As time went on they decided the best thing to do was to give up the baby.

The months passed. The baby finally came, a beautiful baby girl.

The mother left the hospital a few days after the delivery. They kept thinking: a little girl! A little girl! They had two boys. They had always wanted a little girl!

Two days later they went back to the hospital, took the little girl home, and made her their very own.

Now every Sunday the whole family is in church together. The two teenage boys and the "little girl."

One parishioner told the pastor: "If that were my wife, I couldn't have done it. What forgiveness! What a marriage! What a family!"

And what a testimony and witness to that Christian congregation.

How often can one forgive?

> Two small fry have an older brother who is a bully, and he's always beating them up. One day they are coming home from Sunday school, and the lesson has been on when Peter comes to Christ and asks how often one should forgive his brother when he has sinned against him. And Christ replies not seven times, but seventy times seven.
>
> And the two children as they walk along are puzzling over how they can apply that story to their big brother. And one says, "We'll keep a book, and we'll write down in it every time we forgive him."
>
> "Yeah," says the smaller child. "And when it's 490 times he'd better watch out!"

I can't say, humanly speaking, how often one can keep on forgiving someone. Take the husband who continues an adulterous liaison with his neighbor's wife even after he has come back to his own wife, "repented," and she's forgiven him—five times. How often does she take him back? How often can she generate love and affection in her heart for him again? (See Matthew 19:9 and 1 Corinthians 7:15.) But forgiveness is possible through the power which Christ gives us, which we cannot muster up by ourselves.

Corrie ten Boom illustrates this in *Tramp for the Lord,* where she recounts how after the war she met a guard who had been her captor in the Ravensbruck concentration camp, where her sister had died. He came forward after she spoke at a church in Munich, and (though he did not recognize her) said he had been a guard at Ravensbruck, and reached out his hand to her, asking for her forgiveness. For a moment, says Corrie, she hesitated, recalling his cruelty to her sister and those around her. Then, knowing God's warning to forgive or we cannot be forgiven (Mark 11:26) and yet still not feeling the ability to lift her hand towards him, she prayed silently, "Jesus help me! . . . I can lift my hand. I can do that much. You supply the feeling."

And as she woodenly thrust out her hand the current of God's healing warmth flowed through her and out to the former guard.

▸ "I forgive you, brother!" she cried. "With all my heart." Corrie says she never has known God's love so intensely as she did then. But she knew it was not her love, for she had tried and did not have the power. "But it was the power of the Holy Spirit as recorded in Romans 5:5 ' . . . because the love of God is shed abroad in our hearts by the Holy Ghost which is given unto us.' "

That's God's challenge to us. To let Him give us that power to forgive which we cannot create by ourselves. And the alternative is a deadly one: "If you do not forgive others, your Father in heaven will not forgive the wrongs you have done" (Mark 11:26 TEV). Jesus calls us to "love the Lord your God with all your heart, soul, and mind. . . . [and] love your neighbor as much as you love yourself" (Matthew 22:37 TLB). We can begin to forgive—and continue to forgive over and over again, no matter how heinous the offense—when we start to grasp the depth of God's love for us.

It is the profoundness of a love that sent His only Son to the cross to suffer and die in our stead. "This is what love is: it is not that we have loved God, but that He loved us and sent His Son to be the means by which our sins are forgiven" (1 John 4:10 TEV).

It is the kind of forgiveness that wooed and chased and yearned after us even when we were running away from Him—going in the opposite direction from His outstretched hands. "But God has shown us how much He loves us—it was while we were still sinners that Christ died for us!" (Romans 5:8 TEV).

It is the kind of love—in contrast to our own—which not only forgives but forgets—forever!

*I, I am He*
*who blots out your transgressions for my own sake,*
*and will not remember your sins.* (Isaiah 43:25 RSV)

So that you and I have to learn to repeat the little prayer (attributed to O. P. Kretzmann):

O Lord, forgive me the sin of coming back to you and asking forgiveness for a sin You forgave—and forgot—a long time ago!

18

Corrie ten Boom, "thinking of the sea which is never far from a Hollander's mind," says that she likes to think that that's where forgiven sins were thrown: "When we confess our sins ... God casts them into the deepest ocean, gone forever. And even though I cannot find a Scripture for it, I believe God then places a sign out there that says, NO FISHING ALLOWED" (*Tramp for the Lord,* p. 53).

And when we grasp the depth of that kind of love and forgiveness, and know and feel "the love of God ... shed abroad in our hearts by the Holy Ghost which is given unto us" (Romans 5:5 KJV), then we can forgive others again and again and again.

# For Discussion

1. For the sake of complete honesty and to really "clear the decks" does a spouse need to confess *everything* one has done wrong in the past?
2. Was Harry Anderson's confession at the banquet a wise decision? Would you have done it?
3. In "South from Alaska," if you were Doug or Doreen, how would you have reacted to your spouse's confession?
4. To avoid hypocrisy, how much should we share with our admiring friends about our weaknesses and sins?
5. Aren't some horrible sins practically "unforgivable"? If we can't avoid *remembering* a heinous act committed against us, how can we truly "forgive" it?
6. "Maybe God can 'forgive and forget' but humans can't." Do you agree? See Isaiah 43:25; Matthew 6:12, 14–15.
7. What is the nature of God's forgiveness? See Psalm 86:5; 103:11–12; Luke 23:34.
8. How often should one forgive? See Matthew 18:21–35; Colossians 3:13.
9. Read 1 Corinthians 13. TEV translates verse 5 as "love does not keep a record of wrongs." How do we do that?

# Session 2
# Communication

## It's a Secret That Makes Me Laugh—until I Cry

Mary Ann Coburg stared at the psychologist's nameplate on the office door. She was smartly dressed in a soft beige suit, enhanced by a gold bracelet and several dainty gold necklaces.

No wrinkles yet. She took care of herself. Stylish and self-confident at 55, she knew what she wanted out of life.

Some clear answers, for one thing.

A mature man in a 3-piece suit passed her in the hall. He noticed her striking blonde hair and clear blue eyes. He paused briefly as if wondering if he should strike up a conversation with her.

But her taut body deterred him. With a quick jerk she opened the office door and strode into the waiting room.

A neat note on the desk in the waiting room read, "The secretary is out to lunch. Please knock on the doctor's door."

Mary Ann did.

"Come in," a firm voice directed.

Mary Ann entered and saw the counselor sitting behind a massive walnut desk.

Balding, paunchy, 58-ish, with a boyish, puzzled look on his face—he looked as if he'd just been caught robbing the cookie jar.

He began to rise. Mary Ann stared at him. "I'm here for marital counseling," she said.

He settled back in his big leather chair.

"Of course." He paused, and after a brief look at his watch, said, "How can I help you?"

"Well, this husband of mine . . . " Her voice trailed off as she looked at the neatly spaced, framed degrees on the wall of the psychologist's office.

"My husband . . . seems to have lost interest in me."

The doctor didn't move a muscle.

"I need affection," she said. "I know my husband still loves me, but he seems to have forgotten *the way it was.*"

The tune of the song flicked through her brain so quickly that she almost missed snatching it. *The way it was.* Then she let it go.

"I sincerely love my husband," she continued, "but he seems to have forgotten me.

"Oh, we talk, all right. 'Pass the butter.' 'How did your day go?' 'Any letters from the kids?' 'Do you need any money?' You know . . . "

The psychologist shifted in his chair.

"What do you think the *real* problem is?" he asked.

Smug, this man, Mary Ann thought. Undaunted, she continued, "I know I'm no angel, but I think my husband has lost his perspective. He's gotten what he wanted out of our marriage, security of a sort, and kids. But now he's steeped in his work, and . . . "

Her voice trailed off again as she stared at the picture of the doctor's wife on the wall—taken some years before, she thought.

"How can I help you?" asked the doctor.

Mary Ann paused a moment. "How can I get him to understand?" she replied.

"I want him to remember that it's still important to *touch,* to *feel,* to *care.* With more than words! I still desire him."

The doctor looked toward the ceiling, then at the ball-point pen in his hand and the golf trophies above his bookcase.

They talked, long and intensely.

"I know my husband cares for me," Mary Ann concluded. "It's just that he gets so absorbed in his work. I know he's not as young as he was. But all I'm asking for is a little more affection.

"God!" She said it as a prayer. "You don't know what it does to me when he has to get up early to go to the office, leaving me in bed. With his bathroom door open, I smell his cologne. It sifts through the room into my nostrils. Then he's gone and I'm alone in bed, and, oh God! I want him so much . . .

"My friends would never guess this is the biggest problem in my life. I put up a pretty good front. But I never talk about these things. No one would ever guess.

"It's a secret that makes me want to laugh—until I cry."

The psychologist moved uneasily in his chair.

"I . . . " he began.

Mary Ann took the initiative. "Do you think I still have a marriage?" she asked. "I feel like it's only a partnership now."

The doctor didn't reply.

"You haven't really helped me much today," Mary Ann continued.

"You know, I've heard a lot about you from other people," she said quietly, "and they claim you are able to help them more than you are able to help yourself."

Mary Ann stood up. Her trim suit and delicate gold accessories stood out against the walnut-paneled walls of the psychologist's office.

"No marriage—just a partnership," she repeated.

"Is that so bad?" the doctor asked quietly.

"No," Mary Ann replied wearily. "But I had hoped for much more."

She walked out of the doctor's office. The secretary had not returned. Looking at her watch, Mary Ann realized she had been there a very short time.

Closing the office door behind her, she stared at the nameplate again.

James Coburg, Ph.D.

Psychologist.

Her husband.

# The Shave

The bright morning sun that poured through the hotel room window finally awakened him. Julie continued sleeping; her steady breath sounded like a motor humming softly.

His body came to life gradually. His mind cleared. Get up? Go to the bathroom? Stay in bed. One more round of sleep!

He rose. No choice at this age! Forty-six! He rarely made it through the night any more without at least one trip.

In a moment he returned to the bedroom. Not a stir or a sound from his wife. What a woman! Finally, they'd gotten away for their first vacation alone—in years. And to the place they'd always wanted to see: Banff!

As he walked toward the window, he recalled the drive up into the mountains from Calgary, the sweeping views, the grandeur of the Canadian Rockies, and then Banff itself.

He looked down into the little main street below the window. A rush of memories from the previous day flooded his mind.

It struck him that the area resembled an earlier culture in an ageless, peak-ringed valley; every modern convenience was available. He relished the European-accented voices— German, Latvian, Estonian. The fresh, trusting looks of the happy young girls. "Hi!" they called out to him, a total stranger. Their laughing faces danced in front of his eyes— waving blonde hair, leggings, parkas, heavy mountain sweaters.

When he and Julie took their first afternoon's stroll they were struck by the strong angularity of the late afternoon sun. The street names caught their eyes: Otter, Bear, Wolverine. The old, unusually small houses, often made of stones, with glassed-in porches, heavy shutters, had a cozy kind of feeling to them. He had visualized a warm fire and friendly family inside.

They had seen an old Ford station wagon loaded with a week's groceries—flour, powdered milk, other basic staples, in front of a grocery store. He visualized a distant cabin in the mountains, a small, well-knit family growing up in rugged terrain. The young wife, about 23, not too attractive, sat in the front seat waiting patiently for her husband. Two kids, 3 and 6, played "trucks" quietly in the back of the wagon.

*Banff!* What a setting! And always the clouds shifting around the peaks high overhead.

His wife stirred, turned over in bed. His musing stopped, suddenly. Time to shave.

He reentered the bathroom, closing the door softly. Peering at himself in the mirror, he grimaced as he saw devil's horns of hair askew around his bald head. A bit of gray at his temples. That pleased him. A little water to paste that hair down. There. Comb it out. "Not so bad looking now, eh?" Somehow he didn't appear as bald when he looked at himself head-on in the mirror. It was just once a year, when he bought a suit, that he really grew frustrated by those three-way mirrors in clothing stores. It was then he admitted how bright and bare his pate was.

*Did she love him anymore?* That woman—Julie—lying there, sound asleep in their hotel bed. Some woman, that. When the pasty feeling of the inside of his mouth began to assail him he brushed his teeth.

"You don't really love me," he had once accused her.

"I married you, didn't I?" she quickly replied.

That ended that conversation. He yearned for more. "A little affection," he called it.

Again last night. They were on their vacation. Together. Alone for the first time in ages.

"Good-night!" she had said, quietly but firmly, as he leaned over to kiss her.

Crushed, he answered, "Good-night."

He finished brushing his teeth, spit, rinsed. And with wet hands he smoothed the hairs curling on the back of his neck, angling his head from side to side to make sure none of them stood out.

"I love her," he told himself. "Why doesn't she love me the same way?"

He admitted she was a fantastic woman. Always working. Always. During their 20 years of marriage he hadn't met another woman whom he'd rather have as the mother of his six children. Other men admired her. At parties she was never without a circle of admirers.

"Just a little more affection," he pleaded silently.

His mouth, refreshed, felt better. He swallowed several times and ran his tongue over his lips. Next, Williams Lectric lotion. Lime, no less. It cooled his face. He sniffed. Ah . . .

She was always so tired. Sometimes it was go and go all day, and when nighttime came, she'd say "I just don't want to see another person."

"Even your husband?"

"Even my husband!"

"There's been so much going on, I've become so drained; and so many people are *using* me that I have to have a few hours of rest at the end of the day."

He inserted the razor cord in the wall socket.

Yeah, she did give a lot of herself to others. He had to admit that. And the way she lived for their children! Amazing! No complaints in that department.

Yet he ached for something more. He remembered the time, sitting in church, when he had noticed a gray-haired, middle-aged couple, about 55, holding hands. They sat alone in a pew, removed from the crowd. The man was tall, lumbering. Holding hands in church!—at age 55!

He plugged the razor in and began the routine movements just under his right ear.

"You just feel sorry for yourself!" she had once accused him. "Self-pity! That's your problem," she had said. And he had cowered, caught, noting the truth, blanching in the face of it. Later, he had apologized. That was hard, but easy. She had reminded him how easily he said he was sorry.

Hours had passed—night had come and gone. The next morning he knew by the way she flushed the toilet and walked downstairs, by the way she had cleared her throat (if the pitch was high, it was positive, okay), by the way she had walked into the kitchen for her coffee (if it was brisk it was a good signal), and by the way she shuffled the pans on the stove whether or not she had forgiven him again.

He unplugged the razor momentarily. Had the phone rung? No. Utter silence! He always imagined calls and voices when the razor whined and sang away near his ear.

But "just a little more affection!" he repeated to himself. "You don't really need me!" he silently accused her. Sadness tugged at his heart, and he gulped. An old phrase in a church devotional book came to mind: "Better a home where two hearts beat as one in a third floor rear than a palatial mansion where two hearts beat as two."

"Get yourself a mistress!" he recalled when one friend had boozily advised such action. But he couldn't do that. He didn't believe in it. And, frankly, he admitted to himself, he didn't have the guts for it, anyway.

He finished shaving, and with a tiny brush began to fleck out the embedded bits of peppery hair in the razor's head.

Death? He sighed, grieving for himself. Yes, he had thought of death. Then she'd be sorry!

Wow! Instantly he thought of a neighbor of theirs in Virginia who had hanged himself. When the wife called the police and her minister, they found her in the garage, looking up at the swaying corpse, saying, "Oscar, how could you do this to me?"

He could show Julie.

No, he couldn't.

He heard the bed squeak. A smile crossed his face. He snapped his razor box closed, cleared his toiletries from the sink, and stood back, gazing at his reflection.

"Handsome dog!" he said, complimenting himself.

He had decided! *He* would forgive *her*!

He took one long, last look at himself and walked out of the bathroom to begin another day.

# Never the Same Again

Lionel Lochmann pulled his four-door Skylark into the parking lot of Escondido Community Church. Immediately his nine-year-old son, Billy, leaped from the back seat. Slamming the door he headed for the nearby swing set he had spied.

"Billy," Lionel shouted angrily, "Open the door for your mother!"

"It's okay, Lionel," said Valerie. "I don't mind."

27

It's no use, Lionel told himself as they walked past the playground toward the church.

"I *hate* that kid," he muttered to himself.

"Come on, Billy!" Valerie called. "We'll be late for the wedding."

The trio joined about 300 other people entering the good-sized church, signed their names in a guest book in the foyer, and seated themselves in the last empty pew at the rear of the church.

The church was designed "in the round," with pews on three sides facing a free-standing altar. Lionel groaned inwardly. *No cross above the altar!* Hammond organ going full blast—with tremolo yet. Double ugh!

"Give me strength," he whispered to Valerie in his best Dagwood Bumpstead imitation.

"Honey, they're our friends," Valerie responded. "And it's their wedding. But I understand." She gave him a quick hug.

Billy, seated between them, squirmed and said, "Why did we have to go to a church—and on a *Saturday,* Mom?"

"It's a wedding, Billy. Hush now. Look, they're recording the wedding on a videocassette."

To the right of them they saw the monitor, and Billy was quiet momentarily.

As Lionel glanced at his son, the old resentments surfaced again.

He was the child they'd never planned to have. The unexpected. The disaster, actually. Because for the three years before Valerie accidentally became pregnant, Lionel and Valerie enjoyed a perfect marriage.

They were absorbed in each other. Whether they were at the beach or in the mountains, at a party or in a crowded restaurant, it was as if there were only two people in the world—just he and she.

He called her two to three times a day from the Bank of America, where he worked. Walking through the front door of their home after work thrilled him. Always immaculate, Valerie welcomed him with outstretched arms. His cocktail glass already had ice cubes in it. And the dinner was on hold in the oven.

Those three years were heaven on earth, he recalled.

His reverie ended abruptly when Valerie nudged him gently. Slowly, very slowly, the bridesmaids, in soft pastel-shaded dresses, entered from the extreme far right and far left doors at the end of the sanctuary.

Lionel tried to ignore the hackneyed "Tum-tum-te-tum" sounds belching from the organ. Two smiling five-year old girls, their blonde hair neatly combed, followed the bridesmaids arm-in-arm down the center aisle.

Lionel sighed again and slipped back into his reverie.

Valerie. Heaven! Then Billy came. Their relationship was never the same. Something wonderful, indefinable, was lost—never to be retrieved. And Billy, the unwanted, unplanned-for little surprise, had spoiled everything!

He didn't really hate the boy, he thought, attempting to reassure himself. But after Billy came, weekend champagne breakfasts vanished (the kid was always crying in the bedroom). Gone were the solitary, idyllic hours they'd spent listening to their favorite recordings of the Bruch and Wienowski violin concerti. Or the quiet moments tenderly loving each other in bed listening to Khachaturian's *Spartacus*.

And then as the boy matured, more hassles. The constant presence of neighbors' kids in the house, Cub Scout meetings and Little League games. Argh! Lionel moaned, remembering.

Though Valerie sensed their loss, she was patient with the boy. She loved Billy deeply and cared for him tenderly. But he was not a "mommie's boy." Billy was making it, Lionel mused, but not because of him. Valerie exerted the greatest influence.

The two doors through which the bridesmaids had come swung open again, and Lionel, drawn back to the present, watched as the bride and her father entered from opposite sides of the nave.

The father and his daughter exchanged loving glances across the crowded church as they slowly, oh, so slowly, approached each other. Then they met. The daughter took her father's arm and together they approached the altar. It was not only "their" wedding, as Val had said, it was their last walk together as father and child.

"Dad!" Billy whined. "How long is this going to last?"

Resentment flared. "Be quiet!" He mouthed the words silently with livid lips.

"Children destroy" he thought again, quickly averting his eyes from his son.

And the kid always smelled of sweat and the stale sandwiches he brought home. "I bought Twinkies," he'd told Val.

He looked at Val. How he loved her! She had done the best she could these nine years. But it would never again be "the way it was."

Someone dimmed the lights for the pastor's sermon. Another theatrical touch! A spotlight focused on a banner dangling from the ceiling. On it were three words—obviously placed there for the wedding: "Love . . . a Decision."

A *decision?* Lionel frowned. The preacher continued. He addressed the father and the bride, still standing quietly in front of the altar. "You are not 'giving' your daughter away. She was never your possession, rather a trust from God. Are you now willing to turn that trust, that responsibility, over to Barry Cartwright?"

This man was no fool. Good comments! But why that lousy carnation on that three-piece business suit he's wearing? Lionel remembered with nostalgia the dignified worship services of his youth, when the pastor wore a white alb and the appropriate stole for each liturgical season.

"Love is a decision," the pastor repeated.

That doesn't make sense, Lionel thought. Love is a matter of the heart, not of the head. Yet the preacher made sense. Though uneasy, uncomfortable, he heard a Gospel message he hadn't heard for a long time. It hit home!

The past stirred in Lionel's soul. "The Holy Spirit . . . " he heard the pastor say several times. And then, as the short sermon came to an end, he heard the pastor say, "And so . . . will you decide to *outserve* and *outgive* one another? This applies not only to two people in a marriage relationship, but to all persons that God has given as a gift to our families. They are a trust and a responsibility. You children—you parents—you grandparents—you brothers and sisters, will you decide to outserve and outgive each other?"

God knows Val had outserved and outgiven *him* in terms of caring for their unplanned child, Lionel confessed to himself.

Then he looked with new understanding at his son Billy. A *gift* from God. A trust? Yes. A responsibility—as much as his wife.

Lionel looked around the church again. It wasn't like the church he grew up in. But it incarnated truths he had forgotten for too long.

The pastor introduced the new couple—husband and wife. Lionel blinked back a tear. He looked fondly at Val.

" . . . and the Holy Spirit bless you and keep you . . . "

The Holy Spirit. That's what he had missed. And it was here. The same Holy Spirit he remembered learning about in confirmation class when he was young.

The old hymn, "Come, Holy Ghost, God and Lord . . . " drifted through his mind.

I have a decision to make, he told himself. He must love his son, not only in thought but in deed. For "love is always action," not a "motive," the preacher had said.

Billy pulled on his father's coat sleeve. "Dad, is it just about over?"

Lionel looked at the bride and groom who were now facing the congregation. There was a relaxed freshness and joy evident on their faces. Their whole life was ahead of them.

And so was Valerie's and Lionel's—and Billy's.

"Dad, is it almost over?" Billy repeated wearily.

Lionel put his arm around his son and drew him close. "No, Son," he said. "It's just beginning."

# For Discussion

Now let's focus on the thought processes of the characters involved in these stories.

What really motivated them to think they way they did? Are those thoughts ever your thoughts?

1. In "It's a Secret," what is Mary Ann Coburg's next step?
2. When a couple's careers diverge, what are the warning signs indicating estrangement? Similarly, for married or

single persons, what causes friendships to falter or break up?

3. In "It's a Secret," if both a husband and wife refuse counseling, what can be done?

4. What *really* causes "the fire to go out" in the bedroom?

5. Do you feel the man in "The Shave" had "missed the boat"? Aren't there times when a woman's priorities should place her children before her husband?

6. What is the first thing you look for as a man/as a woman in a spouse? How do you prioritize the qualities you desire in a mate?

7. Whether you are single or married, what do you look for most in making a friend? See Proverbs 17:17a; Ecclesiastes 4:9–10; John 15:13; Philippians 4:8.

8. In "Never the Same Again" in what sense is love a "decision"? See 1 John 3:18.

9. What did you think of the pastor's comments? Doesn't "outserving" and "outgiving" one's spouse sound like competition? See Romans 12:9–10; Ephesians 5:22, 25; 1 Peter 3:1–2, 7–9.

# Session 3
# Gossip

## But I Am Still a Virgin!

Tall, regal Ellen Mitchell was known by everyone at St. Paul's Church as totally dedicated to her work as director of Christian education. Maybe that's why there was one person at the church who didn't like her.

Ellen had smiling blue eyes and short, cropped blonde hair that she ran her hand through repeatedly as she talked.

With autumn approaching, she threw herself into the fall educational program. One Monday, Ben Henderson, president of the congregation, asked to see her.

They sat down in her office, and she relaxed for a moment. She was always at ease with him. He was well loved by everyone. "Gentle Ben," they affectionately called him at St. Paul's. He was wearing a new sport coat.

"You look great today, Ben," Ellen said cheerily.

"Well," he chuckled, "you can tell when you get to be my age. That's when your back goes out more often than you do."

Ellen quickly put her hand through her hair and tried an indulgent smile.

But then Ben's mood changed. "I'm sorry I have to say this, Ellen. But Pastor's out of town on that Lutherland tour, and I had to come directly to you. I'll get right to the point."

He shifted in his chair, gave a little cough, and began. "Recall that conference you attended in Walnut Grove with

Pastor Johnson two weeks ago? Erica Ferguson came to me threatening to tell others that on Wednesday night, August 30th, she saw you go into Pastor's hotel room at 11 p.m. *and* saw you coming out again at 7 the next morning."

Ellen's eyes widened. She swallowed hard, as a "this can't be happening to me" bomb exploded inside her head.

Before she could speak, Ben added, "I'm sorry. I don't say I *believe* her. I simply want to be open and honest with you, and I want to help you if I can."

After one slow, long breath, Ellen began her explanation. "I delivered some papers to Pastor's room at 11 p.m., stayed 15 minutes, then left. A little before 7 I was at his door again, as we had agreed, to pick up the papers he had edited, so I could xerox them for a 7:45 meeting after breakfast. Apparently that's when Erica saw me 'come out of Pastor's room.' "

Angry now, she added, "This is horribly unfair, Ben! Pastor can prove it, but he's out of the country for another week. I'll bring in character witnesses! I'll even go to a doctor to prove I'm still a virgin!"

She blushed, and ran *both* hands through her hair, aware that gossips could still say she spent the night in the Pastor's room.

Ben sighed painfully. "I know, Ellen, but rumors are difficult things to cope with. And this—ah, incident—I trust you. Don't misunderstand me. It is complicated by the fact that Pastor likes to play the ladies' man at times. Oh, he means well, but there have been stories. However, I don't believe them."

"Nor do I!" Ellen answered hotly.

And then they talked together, softly, Ellen sitting stunned most of the time, trying to cope with something that had never happened to her before in her whole life.

Finally, Ben said, "Ellen, I thought and prayed about this for some time before I came to you. And my advice is this: The more you protest, the more people will think something did happen. I suggest you resign," he added slowly.

"But that will constitute admission of guilt!" Ellen responded angrily.

"Well, think it over. Let me know if you want to talk with me again. But in the long run I believe you'll see it would be better for all concerned if you leave. Otherwise . . . well, a lot of people will be hurt—not just you."

Crushed, Ellen left the church. She had always enjoyed walking alone. She'd step on the cracks of the sidewalk, touch the trees as she passed. At home she'd scrape the soles of her shoes as she accelerated her walking.

That was what her Daddy, a pastor, always did, she recalled. After he had spent several hours in the church next door to the parsonage on Saturday, getting ready for the Sunday morning service, he'd come home out the back door of the church very quickly. He'd slam the old church door with a bang. Then, with the confident feeling of a job well done and properly prepared for, he'd scrape his shoes on the cement walk as he stepped briskly into the kitchen for Saturday evening dinner.

But now Ellen walked slowly. She remembered Daddy. But she was not happy like he always was. He was gone now. And so was Mother. She was alone.

Her feet stopped.

She heard Ben's voice again, *"Maybe you'd better resign."* Over and over again.

Four days later Ellen arranged to meet with Ben Henderson again. This time she presented several character references and a cablegram from Pastor Johnson corroborating her statements, plus his request that action be delayed until his return.

Ellen and Ben talked, long and painfully. Though Ellen pressed her case, Ben insisted, "Ellen, people will still say, Where there's smoke, there's fire. You'd be better off moving on."

"No!" Ellen replied. "I'll confront Erica, myself!"

"But what can you prove?"

"That I love my job," Ellen cried.

Later, in her apartment, Ellen paced the floor. She loved her home—with the African violet on the dinette table, the fuzzy animals on her bed, her beloved dog, Schatzi, napping in a chair. She eyed the box of old tennis balls that Schatzi loved to chase. She picked one up, tossed it angrily.

Her mind whirled. *If I stay, there'll be more threats, more gossip. If this gets out (I guess it will) Pastor's in a bind, too.*

*He has more to lose than I. A wife and three kids . . . how will it affect them?*

*What shall I do? If I leave, people could still think something happened. No one can unplug Erica's telephone. It's a no-win deal. Catch-22. And I'm the one who loses.*

"Blast it all!" she exclaimed. She stamped her foot. Schatzi yelped and looked at her with a penitent "but what did I do wrong" plea from underneath the shaggy mop of hair.

And then, mentally, she heard a voice: "Vengeance is Mine, I will repay, saith the Lord."

"A lot of help that is," she thought. Suddenly she remembered a luncheon engagement she had had with her friend, Nancy Gregersen, some weeks previously. Nancy was a director of Christian education, at St. Timothy's Church in nearby Reston. Ellen remembered looking forward to their meeting because of a tidbit of gossip she had which Nancy would just *love* to hear.

Nancy was always fun to be with. Plump and jolly, she always referred to herself as "Ms. 5 by 5." After Nancy had finished her chocolate mousse that day, she'd turned to Ellen and said, "Well, you ingrate, why have you kept me waiting? I can *sense* that the fact you finally bought your VW is not the real reason you're here today."

"Well . . . " Ellen teased. And then she did her usual hand-through-her-hair routine and rolled her eyes toward the ceiling.

"I heard Phyllis Ferguson, the choir director at St. Paul's, is pregnant. She's taking a leave of absence from Jefferson Junior High. She'll be in Hawaii for six months and then . . . well, I don't know the whole story, or what she'll do with the child; but she was always so . . . so blasted *self-righteous*. Remember how she acted at that workshop we attended together a month ago?"

"Juicy, juicy," Nancy had exclaimed, licking her lips as well as her dessert.

The conversation had continued with renewed interest until both women glanced at their watches and headed for their cars.

Ellen recalled that as she drove home she felt guilty about what she had said. But that *was* the truth, wasn't it?

And Phyllis had always been so arrogant, so exasperatingly condescending toward her. Oh, she was a proud one!

Ellen blinked her eyes back to the present tense.

And tense it was.

Slowly she ran her hand through her hair. She stared at the tennis ball a few moments. And the truth hit her.

In slow motion, she walked across the room, opened the closet door, and took out her suitcase and began packing.

Vengeance is *Mine,* she thought. The boomerang flew back—hit me!

"*Erica Ferguson.* I teach the kids in Sunday school to love their enemies. And I'm supposed to love *her* now in the face of what she's done to me? I'm supposed to love her! She has not asked for *my* forgiveness for what she's done to me—*as if she would!*

"Where do I go? What do I do?

"And I have to keep my mouth shut."

She threw another batch of undies into her suitcase.

"Blast it!" she moaned. "If I stay, I lose. If I leave, I lose."

She looked out the window. A small yellow bird, perched on the compost heap in the back yard, sang its heart out.

Again, a mental message: If you don't forgive others their trespasses, our Father in heaven will not forgive your trespasses.

"I believe that," she told herself. "But it's so hard . . . "

"Dear God," she muttered, "forgive me! Help me never to breathe another word of gossip about anybody else again."

And then, suddenly, in her mind's eye she could see the woman in the square who *was* guilty and to whom Jesus had said, "I don't condemn you, either. Just don't sin again."

And she knew then that she felt free within herself—like that bird still singing away outside.

At that moment she felt free. In her heart she knew she had been slandered, used. But she no longer hated Erica.

Now, she could stay, or leave, either way. It no longer mattered.

She picked up a tennis ball.

Schatzi, beloved companion, eyed it with anticipation.

She knew he wondered whether she was going to drop the ball into the suitcase—or throw it to him.

# For Discussion

A young boy had spread vicious lies about his classmates around the neighborhood. To teach him a lesson, his father told him to put a feather on the front step of the home of every one of his classmates whom he had maligned. The boy fulfilled the task, and came back exhilarated.

"Now go and pick up each feather," said his father.

"But they will all have blown away!" said the boy. "It's too late."

"Yes," said the father. "And so it is with your words. Once spoken, they cannot be brought back."

1. Does one tell a pastor if he is known to have a "ladies' man image"?
2. To whom is Ellen *primarily* responsible?
3. If you were Ellen, would you stay—or leave?
4. What is the first step in handling rumors in a congregation?
5. Can we always count on God to avenge wrongs done to us? See Romans 12:19–21.
6. Is it right to pray to God to make an actual intervention in a bad situation, or are we rather called to suffer our trials patiently? See Genesis 32:9–12, 25–28; Psalm 88; 94:1–4, 107:1–2, 6.
7. Does God sometimes punish us with trials when we have done wrong to others? See Hebrews 12:5–11.
8. Is it really possible to love an enemy? See Matthew 5:38–48; Mark 11:26; Romans 5:5; 1 Timothy 1:12.
9. Must I forgive someone even if they haven't asked my forgiveness for something they've don't to me?
10. When a person is known to have done evil, isn't it hypocritical to follow Luther's explanation of the eighth commandment: "defend him, speak well of him, and explain everything in the kindest way"?

# Session 4
# Pride

## I'm Sorry

James Ellison Hunt, crack attorney of East Baton Rouge Parish, Louisiana, jumped into the rented car and headed for familiar territory. Memories of the past flooded in on him as he left the New Orleans airport and pointed the car toward the northwest.

A profusion of flowers greeted him on both sides of the highway. But it was a sticky day, and as the air conditioner built up its strength, steam poured out of it. It was 100 degrees, with 98 percent humidity!

He slumped back and drove on, his eyes occasionally casting over to the cypress stumps sticking up snakelike out of the bayou. His mind went back to another time he had lived, not far away, years before.

He recalled those early, happy days with Julianna. The three bouncy children arrived quickly—son Julian, then Melanie Rose and Melissa Kay, the twins. He remembered the summer trips they took together when he took time off from work at his law office. Trips to New Orleans—Antoine's Restaurant—the French Quarter—soft-shell crab—boat trips on Lake Pontchartrain.

But always they returned to his domain, where he, like his daddy and grand-daddy, ruled the roost, and sought to carry on all the grand traditions of his forebears.

Looking back now, he recalled how gradually life had gone sour. The three children left for college at Ol' Miss, met their future spouses and married. They came home rarely after that. He wondered why.

Then he thought of lovely Julianna. How proudly he had displayed his "catch" to his young fellow attorneys-to-be. "A true Southern belle you've got there," they said. She was possessed of a fey nature, and James Ellison Hunt squired her around as a southern colonel would have done in Civil War days.

But his legal practice had always come first. After all, he, the aspiring attorney, was the provider, wasn't he?

So he frequently came home late, proud of his advances in his profession (business first!). Once home he unpacked all his tensions and anxieties on gentle, patient Julianna.

She always listened. He wondered now if she had ever had anything to say; but he couldn't remember.

It was so long ago.

The years seemed to merge. Thirty years seemed like yesterday, and 10 years ago—that must have been the first time she'd said those fateful words. He visualized her now, sitting quietly at the kitchen table. Her gentle, once-shy eyes expressed deep pain. They looked like the quivering eyes of a wounded animal struggling to understand why.

"James," she said that morning, softly, over breakfast— the children were gone now. They were alone.

"James, in all the years we've been together, I've never heard you say 'I'm sorry.'"

Noting the look in his eyes, she gave a scared little cough and continued. "You've never said 'I'm sorry' unless you felt cornered, and *had* to admit some wrong. And then the words were said grudgingly. Yet you still had an ingenious way of saying the words and then projecting your guilt onto me. I could never understand how it happened. Often, even when I couldn't understand what I had done wrong, and you had hurt me so much . . . still . . . I was somehow the one at fault. I still don't understand how it always happened."

That was the way the rubber had met the road in their marriage, he mused. Imagine naive, diminutive, little Julianna questioning him—a successful attorney!

The trouble was, Julianna was usually too easy-going. The few times she did show anger—and, now he conceded, perhaps for valid reasons—she would explode. Later, when she cooled down, she would say she was sorry.

Suddenly he recalled how he'd move in and accuse her of being an "easy-apologizer," a person who got off the hook by just saying "I'm sorry."

He, on the other hand, considered himself a steadfast disciplinarian, priding himself on rarely, if ever, making a mistake that demanded an apology. He had a slow boiling point, but when he finally did explode, it was with righteous anger that often lasted for days.

It was strange how he had the clever ability to get things back on track again. After Julianna had done something wrong, and after he had finally decided to forgive her, he would bound down the stairs to breakfast, eat an especially big meal—complimenting her—and then cheerily leave for work. An uncanny sense told him she felt she was back in his good graces—all was forgiven. He didn't need to *say* he was sorry.

This approach worked on his job, too. He kept people on their toes. Admired and respected, he got results. He admitted he didn't have many close friends, but as the maxim says, It's lonely at the top.

But he could take it.

Then, five years ago, Julianna had left him. Julianna and he had fought over a minor disagreement. He had nagged her, so she said, about spending so many evenings at Baton Rouge University. He expected her to stay home as she always had, and engage in conversation when he— when they—felt like it.

She had quietly insisted on how much the courses meant to her, and he blew up. It was then she said she just couldn't bear his insensitivity anymore and was going to leave him. She was not going to gouge him. Money was not her object. Simple security was enough.

It was not for another man. "I want to find myself," she said simply. "I don't hate you. I don't love you. I just don't feel anything toward you anymore."

He fought her bitterly. "This just isn't done in our family! We're Southerners! Think of the disgrace! What will people think?"

But not once in their conversation, even then, memory told him, did he say "I'm sorry."

Rather, his "justifiable" pride had taken over and he had stormed out of the room.

The next morning, he had bounced downstairs from his bedroom in his usual, forgiving manner. At the foot of the stairs stood Julianna's large, medium, and small suitcases, a coat thrown over them.

He found Julianna in the back yard with her sister Sarah. Sarah's arms were outstretched in a pleading gesture. They stood arguing in the middle of the gazebo.

Then Sarah sputtered, "But you just can't leave your husband! It . . . it . . . just isn't done!"

Julianna, in spite of her petite height, stood with arms folded across her breast in cool defiance.

After a limp Sarah departed, Julianna had left the house as well—in deafening silence.

Brilliant attorney James Ellison Hunt, of East Baton Rouge Parish, Louisiana, had stood in the front room of his well-appointed Southern home, alone, looking out the window at the empty street, vacillating between self-pity and triumph.

For weeks he had attempted reconciliation. But he usually ended up trying to justify himself, and the evening dinners with Julianna ended in disaster. Julianna actually seemed happy and contented away from him—not dependent upon him. That maddened him. How could she do this to him? He felt embarrassed with his acquaintances at the club. Not that they said anything. But he could tell by their looks.

Later, he began to date other women. He thought he charmed them. But in a month or two they excused themselves, saying they were busy or had another engagement. So he had given up. Puzzled, he wondered what he had done wrong. He had always had a way with women.

So he tried travel. London—Amsterdam—Berlin—Rome—Zurich—Paris—Madrid—even Africa.

It had been on his last trip—this time to St. Thomas Island in the Caribbean—that son Julian had left a message at the hotel saying Julianna wanted to see him.

He rejoiced! Now she was ready to come back, he told himself.

His pride inflated, he waited two days before taking a plane to New Orleans. After a quick phone call, he drove to the outskirts of Baton Rouge.

He drove up a winding road. This was where they said to come. The scent of magnolia blossoms filled the air.

He looked down at the huge bank of flowers covering her fresh grave. He wept.

"Julianna, I'm sorry."

# The Young Fireball from the Seminary

"Wow! What a crock!" young Peter Quandt exclaimed as he drove his sporty convertible out of the church parking lot and headed toward home.

Andrea, his wife, did not respond. Instead she sat quietly, looking out at the tall corn stalks with their tassels waving gently in the fall breeze.

Peter had graduated from the seminary three months previously. His first assignment took him to a new mission in a suburb of Lincoln, Nebraska. He and Andrea settled in a small apartment, and, since services in his new church were not to begin for another month, he had made calls on parishioners. Each Sunday they visited neighboring parishes.

Today they attended a country church.

Peter talked on in his usual exuberant way, but this time critically.

"Did you ever see so many weird things at one church, Andrea?

"First of all, as we walked in, the organist was playing 'We Are in His Holy Temple' with the tremolo on. In D flat minor, I'm sure. I thought I was in a funeral home! I began looking for the body!

"Then I heard a clicking sound, and saw an usher punching everybody in with that little gizmo of his. Had to get the right body count, you know!

"Then there were those electric candles on the altar! And that cheap Sallman's *Head of Christ* with its ruby lips and neatly brushed hair. Remember how the usher later explained to us that it was removable, so they could exchange pictures throughout the year!

"And the sloping nave! I wondered when the first feature was to begin. Then those metal plates under the carpet by the lectern and in the pulpit that electronically clicked a spotlight on the preacher when he stood on them. What a gas!

"But the real ringer was that long box over the door next to the pulpit—the box with the numbers 1 to 10 in it. When I asked the usher what it was for, he said, 'Oh, if you're a parent with a child in the nursery, you get a number. If your child acts up, your number goes on.'

"Blink! Blink! Blink!" mimicked Peter. "There's our number coming up, Andrea. Better check on the kid!"

Peter howled with laughter. "Whooeee!"

"But the people were nice and friendly, weren't they, Peter?" said Andrea, softly.

"Yeah!" Peter rushed on, ignoring her question. "But most of all, that old geezer! His glasses looked like the bottoms of Coke bottles! He read his sermon. And the illustrations he used! 'We laugh at children when they play with their paper hats and wooden swords.' That must have come out of a book from 1895—and date back to the Crimean War!

"I couldn't believe what people said when they left the church. They pumped his hand, and said, 'A real masterpiece, pastor!' What fools! I wonder if they know what a good sermon is!"

"Like one of yours, Peter? You . . . a real fireball . . . just out of the seminary?" She laughed, teasingly.

Then she grew serious, and in her usual quiet manner said, "But the Gospel was there, wasn't it, Honey?"

"Well, yeah, I guess it was."

"And although his stories were rather old, I sure got the point he was making from the Bible, didn't you?"

Peter was silent a moment.

"But all those weird little routines they go through in that place!" he countered.

"I know," Andrea responded. "But maybe you and I ought to think twice about that 'perfect church' we're going to have some day. Remember how your professor always reminded your class about the differences in people—the 'difference of gifts', the Bible says. The Holy Spirit can work in many settings—and in various ways."

Again she looked out at the tall corn in long, stately rows. "I believe the Holy Spirit was present this morning. I believe Christ really lives in that man. And those people really love him, don't they, Honey?"

Now Peter was silent even longer. He recalled an old story from long ago, before the days of TV and radio. An actor had given "readings" to a literary club of some kind, and at the end of his performance, someone had asked him to recite the Twenty-Third Psalm.

"Surely, I know that," said the actor quickly. The man delivered the psalm masterfully. His diction was perfect, his timing precise—when it was over, everyone in the hall clapped.

Then someone saw an old pastor standing at the rear of the hall. They asked him if he would recite the Psalm also.

The pastor demurred, saying he wasn't much of a public speaker; but the audience insisted, and so he had begun. His speech was halting, his diction was not clear, but when it was over there was total silence in the room.

Afterward someone went to the actor and asked him, "What happened back there? Why did the people respond so differently? It was the same psalm."

And the actor had replied, "I know the psalm. He knows the Shepherd."

Peter looked straight ahead at the highway leading into Lincoln.

Well, I know the psalm, and I know the Shepherd, he assured himself. But I think I've got a lot more to learn about the Shepherd.

Then he turned to his young wife and remembered the first time he had seen her.

He gradually slowed the car down.

"What's wrong, Peter?" Andrea asked.

He gave her hand a little squeeze, and this time he spoke quietly.

"I hope, some day, I'll be as good a pastor as he is."

# For Discussion

## On Reasonable Pride

*The Voice:*  "After all
I have some pride"
I've always liked
that statement
It has a lot
of integrity
in it
Don't you think so?
We need to retain
our dignity
Not that we should be
arrogant
or insufferable
But certainly
we need to retain
our sense of self-worth
our pride
in ourselves
(When that's gone
what do you
have left?)
I think you can take
pride in your achievements
You have a unique personality
Many people have praised you
over the years

Remember them
Never give up
your self-respect
You too can say
"After all—
I have some pride!"

We speak of "pride in our work," "proud to be an American," "proud of our baseball team." When is "pride" justified and when is it not?

1. Why is it so hard to say "I'm sorry"? See Matthew 15:19; 1 Corinthians 2:14.
2. How can one determine if one is an "easy apologizer"?
3. An actor once summed up his "secret of success" on the Broadway theater circuit: "Act arrogant and talk dirty." Which actors on the TV shows you watch incarnate arrogance and pride? Which ones by contrast show humility? Which one of these two types of persons do people admire the most and why?
4. In what ways did the attorney and the young pastor reveal their pride? What are the beginnings of pride in each one of us? How do we recognize it? See Proverbs 16:18; Luke 18:11; Galatians 6:3; 1 Peter 5:5b–6; Revelation 3:17.
5. What are other ways in which pride asserts itself in our daily lives—in the church? at work? at home?
6. Should you be "proud" of your pastor? Should he be "proud" to be the pastor of your congregation?
7. One congregation, in calling a new pastor, made the following list of qualifications:

He should be energetic and enterprising, yet ripe in experience and wisdom. Not under 40 nor over 45. Married, with a wife that is anxious to help . . . and must be neither too fat nor too thin. He should not be bound to the forms of either high church or low. A good preacher, able to put across his message eloquently and briefly. Devout, yet broad-minded. An inspiration to the flock . . . but just a bit "thick-skinned."

Of such a set of qualifications, one person said: "All that congregation wants is an earthy saint!" Another congregation wanted their pastor to be (1) born in Bethlehem; (2) work for nothing; and (3) stay forever.

What does Scripture mean by "the difference of gifts"? What are its implications for our life together in a congregation? See 1 Corinthians 12.

8. What minimal, basic standards can one expect of a pastor? What personality traits or limitations of ability can one justifiably overlook? See 1 Corinthians 4:1; 1 Timothy 4:6; 2 Timothy 2:15; 4:2; Titus 1:7–9, 2:1.

9. A study has shown that when a congregation and its pastor drift apart, 95 percent of the time it is not because of false doctrine, embezzlement of church funds, adultery, alcoholism, etc., but because of mixed expectations. Would you agree?

What is the pastor's role? In *Lutheran Partners* (July/August 1989, p. 30) Virgil Thompson suggests that the office of the ministry involves Word and Sacrament *and nothing beyond that*. Do you agree?

# Session 5
# Temptation

## Bus Ticket

Chris walked down Panoramic Way, down the Berkeley hills, and looked out over the scene on the Bay. It was late afternoon, and a tubelike funnel of fog drifted past the Golden Gate. Then it would pass Alcatraz, and in another hour be spreading over the East Bay hills.

Here and there a steamer moved imperceptibly across the sunbathed water. Farther to the southwest, he could see planes circling over the airport below San Francisco.

As he walked, Chris was almost heady with anticipation. He had it all planned. This was the weekend he'd been waiting for. He'd finally know. The hunger and the thirst inside him . . .

It was really quite a simple plan. His folks of course had hoped for his usual weekend trip home to Fresno. "But there was this buddy, see, he'd wanted me to come up to Placerville all year, and well, Mom, so I promised him I'd come up for this weekend."

But instead he was going to walk on down Panoramic Way, past sorority row, take the bus down College Avenue and then on down to the busy depot in Oakland. Tomorrow, after that last semester exam, he could catch the bus on San Pablo Avenue. But the driver had chewed him out so much last time he tried to buy his ticket on a bus that he'd rather

51

have it ready—even if it meant this extra trip tonight to Oakland to get the ticket.

And then it would happen . . . as if it had been planned to happen for many years . . . as if the events and the things he would say and do were linked by some invisible chains and pulleys to an immense, grinding clock that went on and on and you couldn't stop it.

He had met Carol in the Bear's Lair on campus at Cal. She seemed detached at first—strong and aloof. But in the easy conversation of mutual friends they had met, and had come to spend many of their between-classes hours together. She was a soc major and seemed to possess all the subtle wiles a coed could have. Her very detachment incensed him, and drew him to her in a kind of compulsion to break down her reserve.

And she too had been taken by this tall, handsome chem major, with his boyish smile and easy, friendly manner. Her almost cold appraisal of most young men who surrounded her in the campus routine had been warmed by the naive friendliness of this lonely looking young student.

And so they had talked, and walked, and sat on the grass below the Campanile on afternoons. And on Sundays they tramped far up Strawberry Canyon and through the Botanical Gardens. And at times he would put his head in her lap and talk of his drive and desire to be a good chemist and teach someday, if he ever finished the grind of school.

And then, as the days went by, he found himself looking at her face in the mirror instead of his own when he shaved in the morning. And then he would blink and realize he was dreaming again . . . And she would give him those little glances, and he could just *tell* she liked him, and was drawn to him. Sometimes she would straighten his tie, or take his hand first, when they were walking, or look up at him when he held her, and laugh, hard and deep.

And then she asked him. Asked him to come up to her folks' home in the Valley of the Moon, the weekend when finals were over, at semester break. Her mother was in the East, her father was gone most of the day. They would swim, and read, and listen to her favorite tapes—and at night they would sit up on the hills and look out over the valley. And somehow, when she talked, he knew—he knew what she

53

meant, and what would happen as that great clock ground on and on, and pulled them on with it.

And he would get his ticket, and tomorrow he would walk out of that test—and feel like yelling, but he wouldn't—and soon he'd be on that bus out of San Pablo—and then—the Valley of the Moon, and she would be there. And a deep yearning and hurting seemed to well up and almost burst inside him.

Chris ran the last half block as he approached College Avenue. It really irked him whenever he just missed a bus. But there was one coming a few blocks away. When it arrived, he boarded it and slowly edged his way down the aisle. As a kid, it used to embarrass him to face a strange group of people like this—going into a restaurant or some place where they would all look at you as if to say, "What are you doing here?" Then his friend Bob had told him just to mentally ask them the same question, and look right back at them. And it worked.

The ride to Oakland would take about half an hour. Outside he noticed they were passing a small, vine-covered church. It didn't look like a church. He'd heard it had quite a history—pagan cult's temple, liquor-running, a murder and suicide. A blonde girl entering a nearby house caught his eye. His heart missed a beat—for a moment he thought it was Carol. But she turned her head. It was someone else.

A twinge of guilt swept over him as he thought of what he was going to do. Somehow, deceiving his folks seemed almost as bad as what he was sure would happen on the weekend at the Valley of the Moon. The bus inched past Ashby, toward Oakland, and he thought of his parents.

They were steady, faithful, loving people. They had always given him love and affection. Yet, somehow, here at school he had been depressed, deeply lonely, aching for the love of someone. His childhood had been quite happy. Why did he get so blue at times?

There was his room at home in Fresno. All his "things" that he treasured—still there in place when he went home weekends. He could read, or play the piano, or just horse around. His folks were always there, accepting him, loving him for just what he was.

And then there was Aunt Helen's. Just three blocks away. And on Sundays they would go over for noon dinner. In the afternoon he would lie down on the floor and turn on the radio and listen to the symphony. Then, later in the afternoon, their favorite programs would begin. And then Aunt Helen would heat over that delicious chicken and green peas, and lots of milk, and she would smile, and self-consciously spread her hands as she straightened her dress and asked if she could get you anything more.

Afterward they would all go over to church for the evening service. There was something he would never forget about those evening services. The attendance wasn't large, but there was a warmth and closeness with the people. The candles, the familiar hymns and liturgy, the quiet voice of the minister. "I am crucified with Christ; nevertheless I live. Yet not I, but Christ liveth in me." He could still hear the minister saying those words in so many of his sermons. It must have been his favorite passage.

But this was another world, here at school. It was a quick, fast-moving world. Everything in Fresno seemed to be like a compartment, a box, which you just could draw out and look at at times, and then close the drawer again. But it wasn't life. It wasn't real. It wasn't here and now, and the gnawing, restless hunger that one had to be loved, and to love, and to know once for all the completion of one's existence.

Chris shook with a start as he heard a red-faced man sitting near him lean over and say with a leer, "I tell ya, if I didn't have a date tonight, I'd pick up something on this here bus!" He looked at the man noncommittally, then looked around the bus. He hadn't noticed, but it had filled with occupants by now. He could overhear the conversation of a group of girls sitting near him: "Do you like your roommate?" "Yes, she's very nice." . . . "If I get good grades, my father will give me a car."

The Valley of the Moon. Why wasn't it right? Why did God have to make a man with a heart sick inside him to be loved, and then say it was wrong? I didn't make myself! And Carol—she seemed so sure of herself. She didn't seem to be bothered by any questions of guilt or anxiety about things. She seemed so sure and confident and right about everything. And yet religion didn't seem to have any part in her life.

Chris suddenly noticed that he was near the bus station. He pulled the cord. Others also rose and got off the bus with him. The street was jammed with traffic, and he twisted his way through the crowd to find the ticket window.

A heavyset man was standing by a rack of books, studying the lurid jackets on their covers. A beautiful red-haired girl stood beside her baggage on the edge of the crowd. A porter roughly pushed past with a cart loaded with bags.

Chris found the ticket line and noticed about three people ahead of him. Standing, waiting, Chris heard two young boys nearby talking loudly, laughing and gesturing. Beyond them a small, thin woman stood smoking vigorously, yelling at her two children. The one, about 12, was poker-faced, the younger one, about 7, was crying broken-heartedly. All three were shabbily dressed and, as Chris watched, the trio became the center of attention of many of the people standing and waiting in the bus station. As the smallest child continued to cry, the mother shouted at her and roughly boxed her ears. The older child looked on stonily.

"One ticket to Napa," he heard the man say in front of him. Chris got his money ready. No one in the bus station did anything about the mother hitting and yelling at the child. It cried on fearfully. Chris would have liked to take it in his arms and then say something, something hard and bitter, to the woman. Then, quickly, the thought flashed across his mind of the story of the soldier who dreamed he saw someone whipping Christ, and when he rushed forward to stop the person, the whipper turned and the soldier saw— himself.

The man in front of Chris stepped aside with his ticket, and Chris stepped forward, leaning on the counter. The clerk didn't even look up, but continued to make notations in a large ledger. At last he turned his face up to Chris.

"Round trip to Fresno," said Chris.

As the clerk reached for a yellow ticket stub and stamped it deftly, Chris half smiled to himself. The folks would be surprised to see him. And as for Carol—well, he'd think of something to tell her.

# For Discussion

1. Given Chris' fine upbringing, wasn't the temptation he faced not of his own doing? See Proverbs 23:7; Matthew 6:21.
2. Who tempted whom? Who's more to blame in the planned tryst—Carol or Chris? See Genesis 3:1; 2 Corinthians 2:11; James 1:13–14; 2 Peter 3:17.
3. Why do you think Chris changed his mind? What do you think moved him to purchase "the winning ticket"? See Deuteronomy 6:7; Proverbs 22:6; Ephesians 6:4; 2 Timothy 1:5.

*Talking About . . . Overcoming Temptation*

A Sunday school teacher had just explained that God never tempts us. But God does *test* us, she said, to make us realize our need for Him and our dependence on Him.

"Any questions?" asked the teacher.

"Yes," said an eighth grade boy. "I know that God only tests us to strengthen our faith. But I still think that sometimes He overdoes it!"

God tests us at times—in love—to strengthen our faith in Him. But we are also *tempted*—by Satan, by our sinful flesh, and by the world around us.

4. What do the following warnings tell us about temptation? 1 Peter 5:8–9; Matthew 15:19; 1 John 2:15–17.

What is one of the easiest ways we can fall into temptation? See 1 Corinthians 10:12.

Overconfidence can be a major reason we succumb to our three tempters. Have you ever heard someone say, "Well, I never would have thought it of *him!*" Or "I wouldn't have believed it, but did you hear what *she* did—and got caught?" "How the mighty have fallen!" And there's a secret kind of gloating satisfaction as we see the feet of clay of the once-proud person.

Yet "there but for the grace of God go I!" Yes, temptation is common to us all. And anyone can fall.

You may think your temptations are unique, but your

fellow believers are going through the very same kind of trials. Believers in God have discovered that by the forgiving power of Christ and the presence of His Holy Spirit, their problems can be overcome. They may not be eliminated, but they can be surmounted. They will no longer crush us, because God keeps His promises.

5. What special promise has God given us? See 1 Corinthians 10:13.

What a wonderful God we have! At times our temptations are so strong that we doubt God's care and concern for us. But God always loves us and helps us by revealing Himself to us in His Word and Sacraments. We should not ignore or resist these means of grace but use them joyfully with an open mind and a penitent heart.

6. What do each of the following verses tell us about God's promises to us in overcoming temptation? James 4:2b; Deuteronomy 33:25b; 33:27; Isaiah 41:10.

The key to our daily overcoming of temptation rests in trusting God and in looking for that "way of escape." Search Scripture, relive your Baptism, and joyfully receive Holy Communion whenever it is offered. Prayer, the counsel of a fellow Christian, and working with all our minds and hearts to simply run away from temptation are further gifts from God to help us resist temptation.

Sometimes the "way of escape" is practicing how to say no to Satan, the world, and our flesh. God promises He will give you that strength.

The Law says, "You can't fool God."

The Gospel says, "You don't have to!"

Avail yourself of His loving power in overcoming temptation. His mercy—His "way of escape"—is always open to you. And receive the power of the Holy Spirit, which our Lord wants to give to each of us.

# Session 6
# Work

## The Firing

George Stryker sat across the table from his sales manager, Ed Reese. Ed did not know it, but George was going to have him fired today. Oh, the word would come from the East, and Ed would never know George had engineered it. But Ed would lose his job all the same.

They were sitting in, of all places, the dining room of a Roman Catholic convent south of San Francisco. Ed was going to attend a one-day laymen's retreat there. As George dropped him off, Ed had talked George into stopping long enough for a cup of coffee. Finally George had agreed; he couldn't take his car to the repair shop in San Francisco until eight anyway. So he had a little time to kill.

Faithful Ed. George watched him sip his coffee. He was 55, a little paunchy, but his blue eyes twinkled as he talked with you. You could always count on him. He was competent, hard-working, a truly honest man. There just was no guile in him. He radiated goodness.

And that's why George hated him. Somehow when he was with Ed, he felt dirty. Ed wouldn't go along with any of the shady deals he cooked up. "It's just not ethical, George," Ed would tell him. "I just can't do it."

But you had to cut corners in this world to get ahead. It was a dog-eat-dog business. Survival. More than that, success. Being at the top. That's what it was all about.

And George had made it. A little older than Ed, he was nearing 60 now. Tall, powerfully built, with a shock of elegantly silvering hair, George knew he incarnated the businessman who had arrived. And he had done it alone. Sure, he'd destroyed people on his way up the ladder. But that's what you had to do. Be ruthless. Think of Number One. After all, one had to be realistic.

George looked at his watch. 7 a.m. Time to head for the City. He smiled benignly at Ed.

"Well, enjoy your 'spiritual retreat,' or whatever it is, Ed," he said expansively. "I've got to head back to the salt mines."

"Thanks for dropping me off, George," Ed replied, smiling and rising. "I'll see you early tomorrow morning at the office."

*Oh, no you won't!* George said to himself, taking Ed's hand and shaking it warmly. Ed should have his pink slip by 2 p.m.

George left the dining room and headed down a long hallway toward a flight of stairs. It was a big old convent, built about 50 years ago. But with fewer sisters entering the sisterhood, and some leaving, the once-filled convent had nearly emptied. Now it was used largely as a conference and retreat center.

Ahead of him George overheard an elderly woman, evidently a sister, but dressed in street clothes, speaking to some new arrivals.

"Oh, you will love it here," she was saying. "Mass is at 7:20 if you are interested. I'm on retreat for a week. I always come 'home' here for my retreat. I was one of the first postulants here in 1947!"

She beamed, but then her face clouded. "I've just come back from El Salvador. Four of the sisters in our order were raped and murdered there a few years ago, you know."

George turned a corner in the hallway and passed by another group. One man was explaining to another, "We're with the Congregational Christian Church. We're working on putting more gays and lesbians into our pulpits."

George passed an open door. Inside were what appeared to be chiropractors' tables. On the wall was a bulletin board announcing:

61

9:00 a.m. BODY TONE THERAPY—Oak Room

9:00 a.m. LUTHERAN PASTORS PREACHING WORK-SHOP—Pine Room

9:00 a.m. NATIONAL COUNCIL OF CATHOLIC FAMILY LIFE ADMINISTRATORS—Cypress Room

10:00 a.m. METHODIST WOMEN CLERGY—Walnut Room

George looked inside at the rubbing tables again and winced. More touchy-touchy, feely-feely, he mused cynically.

He passed a sister slowly wobbling down the hall with her walker. "Good morning!" she said cheerily, beaming up at him.

George grunted a response, but then glanced through another open door. The chapel. He paused momentarily. It was so long ago. He hesitated briefly, then walked through the door. He glanced at his watch. He still had plenty of time. He was more curious than interested. He looked around the nave of the large chapel and seeing it nearly empty, took a seat in a rear pew.

It had been such a long time. George had been a Catholic in his youth, even an altar boy for awhile. But he had given that all up. Turned Methodist. That was the way to get ahead in the business world. Church connections helped. Gave you sort of a respectable image, you know.

But this was different from the Protestant churches he had attended occasionally over the years. They usually had the aesthetic appeal of an old library, and the services seemed like raucous town meetings.

He looked around at the quiet sanctuary. Warm, amber light glowed from the chancel. It was bare. Obviously a renovation of some kind was going on. A simple altar occupied the center of the chancel between two banks of choir stalls that faced each other. A little sister who must be in her 70s was placing a few simple bouquets at the foot of the altar. Getting ready for the service, he thought.

George ran his fingers along the soft brown wood of the pew. Ah, the history and the mystery of the mass! The smells and bells of his youth! He would stay a few minutes. Just a few minutes.

One by one the sisters were entering the chapel now. Each one would come before the altar, genuflect, and then quietly kneel in one of the choir stalls facing the altar. Very few wore habits. A little old bent-over nun was preparing the Communion vessels on the altar. He remembered a commercial he'd seen on TV, of an erect, middle-aged woman helping a crunched-over lady getting off a train. "One day you'll be that woman," the voice-over was saying. "Take our pills. Strengthen your bones now!"

The sisters were an interesting lot. He began to name them as they came in. There was the I-Love-to-Hover-around-the-Altar Nun. The Flowers Nun. The Praying Nun. Well, they were all praying.

He studied the looks on their faces. There was the Mother-Hen Nun. The Teacher-Type Nun. The Impassive Nun. The Tired-Looking Nun. The Ladies Aid-Type Nun. One must be The Sewing Nun, and The Kitchen Nun. He'd often wondered if they had become nuns because they knew they weren't beautiful and probably would never marry.

And then—well, here came The Jogging Nun. A young woman of about 30, dressed in a jogging suit, entered, genuflected, and quietly took her place in one of the stalls.

Suddenly there was a rustling in the chapel, a door opened, and the priest entered. George rose involuntarily, transfixed by the moment. Immediately a lilting chant began from the sisters. It started softly but then rose and soared as George felt the brush of angels' wings down his back.

Ah, the Singing Nuns, he mused, with cold reason trying to pull himself back from the mystical world into which he was irresistibly being drawn.

*I shall rejoice when I go up to the house of the Lord,* the delicate voices were chanting.

George took a deep breath and steeled himself.

The gentle, melodic voices ascended still higher, it seemed almost to heaven itself. He could see now why Ed liked going to church.

*I go up with joy to the house of the Lord! Christ is the source of our hope and our salvation!*

The priest was walking reverently toward the altar now. He strode with dignity, adjusting the heavy green wide-banded stole around his neck. He genuflected and then took his place behind the altar, facing the center of the nave. On his right and left the sisters' chant softly faded away, and they faced him expectantly.

George eyed the priest. Typical ruddy-faced Irishman, about 65. Gray hair. He recalled an old priest he had seen once readying the altar for mass. He had been wearing a soiled T-shirt, shiny black trousers, and scuffed loafers. His hair was disheveled. He went to the john just like everyone else, George mused condescendingly.

The priest spoke warmly to the little congregation.

*Joy and peace to each of you as you begin this day! Christ is the source of our hope. In the Holy Sacrament he will come to us and empower us to live as his loving children.*

*Let us begin by opening ourselves up to his Holy Spirit.*

The sisters began chanting again, this time the age-old Kyrie that George remembered so well.

*Lord, have mercy upon us.*
*Christ, have mercy upon us.*
*Lord, have mercy upon us.*

The priest continued:

*May our God have mercy on us, forgive us our sin, and lead us to life eternal.*

Then he began a prayer calling for the presence of the Holy Spirit.

The nun he had seen earlier was now almost doubled over in her stall, her walker nearby. The Jogging Nun brushed her sweaty brow with her left wrist.

The priest seated himself and sat stolidly, taking on the look of a silent statue in an ancient cathedral.

Now two sisters read lessons from the Scriptures.

*This is the Gospel of the Lord,* each ended.

*Praise be to You, Lord Jesus Christ,* responded the sisters.

The priest arose, and began some prayers.

*We pray for all in this community, and for all on this planet . . .*

Planet? I guess ours is a planet, George mused.

*Welcome into Your kingdom, O Heavenly Father, our departed brothers and sisters, and all who have left this world . . .*

64

The priest paused. He looked at the sisters, and then, George felt, directly at him.

*In the Holy Gospel we hear Christ calling to us to be like Him. We are unloving, self-centered. He calls us to self-denial, as He gave Himself for us by dying on the cross for our sins.*

He paused.

*Our Lord incarnated goodness. Like light coming into a dark place, He showed the evil in people's lives. They hated Him for it. And that's why they killed Him. To follow Christ we must submit to His purification if we are to be filled with a double portion of His Spirit. He forgives us when we repent. He wants to give us a new life, because He loves us so much.*

Something stirred inside George. He eyed the stations of the cross on the walls of the chapel. The priest was consecrating the elements now. He could hear the wine gurgling as it was poured. Then the priest communed himself. George could distinctly hear the host crunching as the priest chewed it in his mouth.

*Come, for all things are now ready,* he said.

The priest invited the nuns to the table with outstretched arms. Immediately they responded,

*Lord, I am not worthy to receive You, but only say the word and I shall be healed.*

"I am not worthy." George rolled the words around on his tongue. "Not worthy?" He remembered his old priest once sighing wearily and confiding to him that hearing nuns' confessions was like being pelted with popcorn.

Again a plaintive chant arose. First just one voice began, then others joined in and the chorus swelled and grew and grew until it ended, beautifully expanding into three blended parts. The nuns began filing towards the altar.

For a moment the sun burnt through the morning fog outside, and a bright shaft of light burst through a high window and shone directly on George. He blinked.

He felt like Scrooge on Christmas morning, his skinny legs dancing on the floor as he realized he had one more chance.

He saw Scrooge throwing the shutters open and calling down to a boy on the snow-filled street.

"Say, boy, is that big turkey still there in the window of the butcher's shop on the corner?"

"Well, I should say it is, guv'nor," says the boy brightly.

"Well, go and fetch it then and here's some money for your trouble." Scrooge throws down a small purse, the boy picks it up, says "Whoosh!" and flies away. And Scrooge dances a jig as a joyful tune taps in response in the background.

"I *will* change!" George jubilated. He cocked his head. "I *will* do better! Why, people won't recognize me for the new person I will be. 'Good old George!' they will say."

Of course he would be very humble about it. They hadn't really known him before. The loving, self-giving guy he really was. A feeling of peace and self-satisfaction surged through him. They would talk glowingly about him behind his back. "Good old George!" He beamed inwardly at the prospect.

*This celebration is ended,* the priest was saying. Quickly, the mass had concluded.

The priest cast a loving look out over his little flock.

*Go in peace and joy!* he exclaimed.

*Thanks be to God!* chorused the sisters.

Stunned, George slipped out of the rear door of the chapel and headed down the hall again.

He was outside in a moment. The sky, now cleared of fog and crystal blue, saluted him. His heart exulted. He strode briskly to his Lincoln and paused. 7-1-8-2-4 He tapped the numbers firmly on the door and heard its automatic opening click. Slipping into the soft leather seat he turned the key. The car sprang to life and the dashboard lit up like the cockpit of a 747.

Well, that had been a curious diversion. But back to the real world. He had that phone call to make. Ed should get his pink slip around 2 p.m.

He headed his car for Highway 101 and the city. It was back to business as usual.

But then as he drove, he wondered.

# For Discussion

1. Why do you think George hated Ed?
2. What really made George consider "turning around" his life?

3. Do you think George will fire Ed Reese?
4. Thinking of one's family security, are there ever times when sheer survival justifies a "shady deal"? See Deuteronomy 24:14; Psalm 82:3; Matthew 6:19–21, 19:23–24; Luke 3:14; Colossians 4:1; Philippians 4:11; James 1:27, 4:4, 13–16; 1 Timothy 6:17; 1 John 2:15, 17.
5. Why do people find it so hard to make a real commitment to change their lives? Consider the following survey conducted by Ministers Life Insurance company:

> Some years ago a survey of businessmen posed the question: "How much guidance did your church and clergyman provide for ethical problems you and your associates faced in the last five years?" "None" said 35 percent. "Some, but not enough"—25 percent. "About right amount"—16 percent, and "Can't say"—23 percent.
>
> Lack of communication is the problem, according to Donald W. Shriver, Jr., of North Carolina State University. The businessman sees the clergyman as: Living in a world of mere ideas; never met a payroll; language that no one else understands; apt to be strangely critical of American way of life.
>
> And as the clergyman sees the businessman: Unaware of the role of ideas in his own business activities; careless about the past and anxious about the future; uses a hard-to-understand economic language; likely to be uncritical of the American way of life.
>
> Low-key discussions between ministers and businessmen offers promise of breaching barriers and resolving ethical conflicts. (*Life Line*—Ministers Life)

6. Is an "emotional" decision a valid reason for returning to the church?

# APPENDIX

*For use as a follow-up for "The Perfect Couple."*

Harry and Betsy Anderson found the secret of a lasting marriage—forgiveness. But they knew the real clue to their victory was not just in giving and receiving forgiveness from each other, but from God. For He is the one we must ultimately reckon with in our lives. "Whatever you have done unto one of the least of these My brethren, you have done to Me" (Matt. 25:25 KJV). And we cannot create the power to forgive or be forgiven from within ourselves.

Our Creator God is the one we have sinned against, and we need *His* forgiveness. Jesus Christ, God's Son, died on the cross to pay for our sins of self-centeredness and self-absorption. He alone can turn your hopelessness into hope. He alone can give you the miracle of a fresh start and do that in your life which you are unable to do in and of yourself.

Now at this point I do not suggest a simplistic formula like "accept Jesus Christ into your heart and everything will turn out all right." Getting to know Jesus as the *source* of forgiveness and beginning a different, new way of living takes some real concentration—as does any worthwhile task. It will mean getting acquainted with Him afresh in the Scriptures. Read the Gospel of Mark first—in a modern translation. Then read the letter of Paul to the Romans. It will be helpful to ask a practicing, authentic Christian to help you along your joyful path of discovery. You can't be a Christian in a vacuum.

You may have been disappointed in your relationship with people in the church. Sure, we have some hypocrites among us, as does every organization. But we have sinners also who admit their need for help outside themselves, and strive each day to live within God's gracious acceptance and forgiveness. We have hope because we are dependent on *His* power, and not our own.

*For more information on the one who does the forgiving, Jesus Christ, and on fellow-strugglers who have found the peace that only God gives, write the Christian Service Center, The Lutheran Layman's League, 2185 Hampton Avenue, St. Louis, MO 63139-2983, or phone 1-800-7-LAYMEN.*

# ACKNOWLEDGMENTS

### About This Book

J. Russell Hale was quoted by Donald L. Deffner in *The Compassionate Mind: Theological Dialog with the Educated* (St. Louis: Concordia Publishing House, 1990), pp. 37–38.

### Session 1

"The Perfect Couple" appeared originally in *The Lutheran Witness* 103:2 (February 1984), copyright © 1984 by Donald L. Deffner.

The story of the "two small fry" is from *You Say You're Depressed?* by Donald L. Deffner (Nashville: Abingdon Press, 1976), p. 44.

Read the whole account of Corrie ten Boom's encounter with her former guard in *Tramp for the Lord,* chapter 7, "Love Your Enemy" (Old Tappan, N.J.: Flemming H. Revell, 1974.)

### Session 4

"On Reasonable Pride," from *I Hear Two Voices: Struggling with Temptation,* by Donald L. Deffner, copyright © 1983 by Concordia Publishing House. All rights reserved.

### Session 5

"Bus Ticket" appeared originally in *This Day* 14:2 (October 1962), copyright © 1962 by Concordia Publishing House. All rights reserved.

"Talking about . . . Overcoming Temptation" appeared originally in *The Lutheran Witness* 105:8 (August 1986), copyright © 1986 by Donald L. Deffner.

Also, my thanks go to David Owren, Tracey Blanchard, Peter Garrison, Dirk van der Linde, Mary Ann Berry, Margaret J. Anderson, Jan Sheldon, Gloria Smallwood, Micheal Kroll, Jeffrey Walther, Becky Kieschnick, Jessica Wilmarth, and Earl Gaulke.